This commemorative booklet and DVD marks the
500th anniversary of the **Battle of Flodden.**

On the 9th of September 1513 around fifteen thousand men perished in the Battle of Flodden. It was the largest battle between England and Scotland, and its repercussions were felt across Europe.

Flodden is arguably the most important event in Borders history. Its legacy reaches across the ages to influence the identity and culture of Borderers and it continues to resonate in communities across Scotland and northern England.

This book is dedicated to the brave of both nations.

We must never forget.

We drink a toast to James IV King of Scots. To his character, his leadership and his outstanding bravery.

We drink a toast to the Border men who fell and to their bereaved families.

We drink a toast in the silence that they left on Flodden Field.

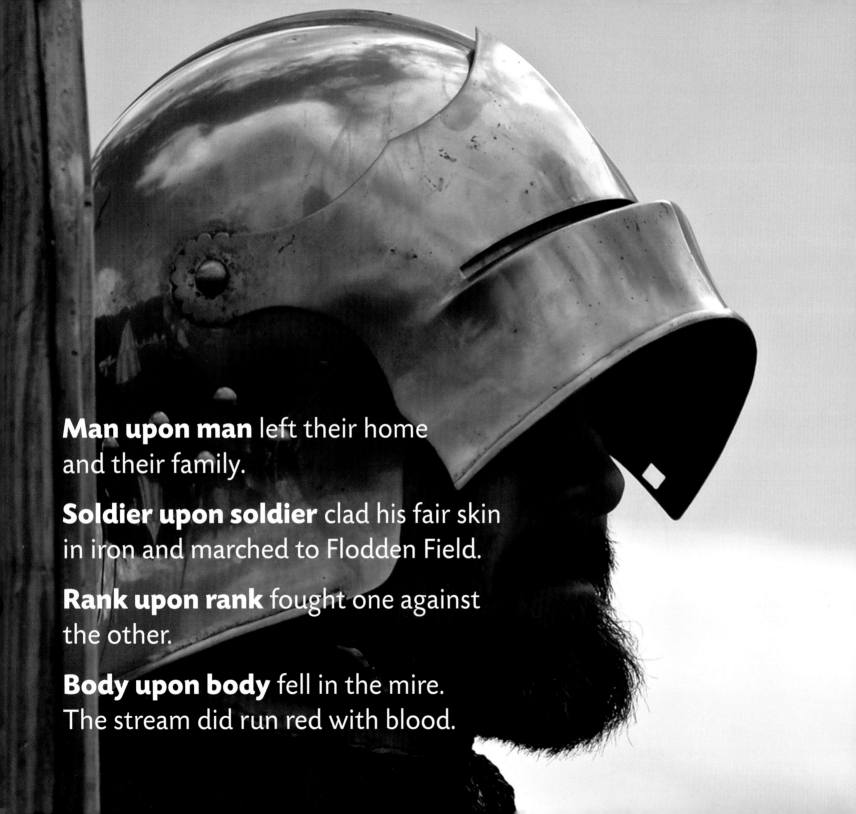

Man upon man left their home and their family.

Soldier upon soldier clad his fair skin in iron and marched to Flodden Field.

Rank upon rank fought one against the other.

Body upon body fell in the mire. The stream did run red with blood.

The Borderers' Return

To commemorate the 500th anniversary, the Common Ridings joined together to form **The Borderers' Return**. Riders carried the Flodden 1513 Standard through nine different Border towns.

Leaving Flodden Field they rode for four days carrying the standard one hundred and thirty miles. On the last day they arrived in Coldstream to hold a remembrance service at the town's monument in honour of the battle.

> *The Borderers' Return is to symbolise the soldiers who did make it home from battle.*
>
> Grant Campbell, Coldstreamer

"

Through transcribing, the battle really comes to life. It really comes home how many people died . . . the pointlessness of war.

Alan Urwin, Transcriber

> "This is an opportunity for members of both sides of the border to work cooperatively to re-discover their history and lay to rest some of the myths that have grown out of the Battle of Flodden.

John Nolan, Archaeologist

> "The aim is to protect the burials of the soldiers who died here. We hope the government will make this land a Scheduled Ancient Monument – the highest level of protection possible.

Chris Burgess, Archaeologist

Remembering Flodden

"

A group of actors got together to put on the first re-enactment of The Battle of Flodden to mark the 500th anniversary.

Ian Shields, Member of The Border Clansmen

“

As a performance historian, to be invited over here to perform this show is immensely important, as Flodden is a battle that often gets overlooked; I have the opportunity to bring the history to life and to a wider audience.

John White, Performance Historian

Weapons

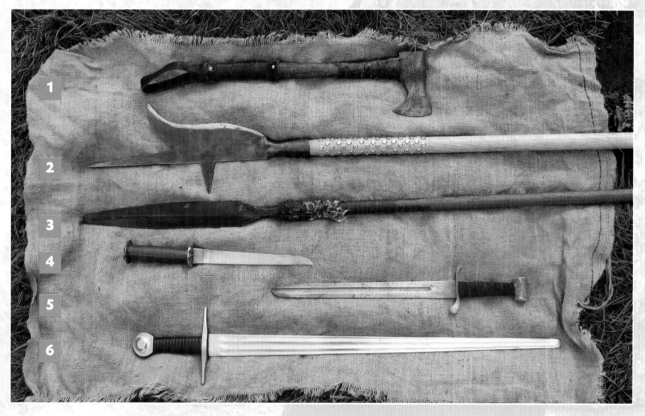

1 Axe
2 Bill Hook

3 Pike
4 Rondel Knife

5 Dagger
6 Single Handed Sword

A red phone box is located on the village green in Branxton.

It is claimed to be the smallest visitor centre in the world, is always open, and attracts thousands of visitors each year.

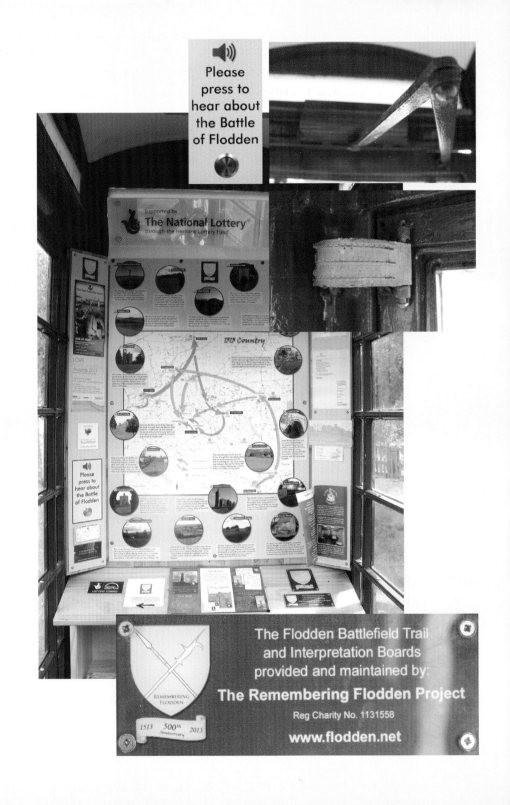

> **"**
>
> *Flodden is a vital part of our history and heritage; one afternoon, five hundred years ago today, this was the centre of Europe.*
>
> Clive Hallam-Baker, Chairman of Remembering Flodden and founder of the Flodden Visitor Centre

> *What happened here is often overlooked and forgotten, and it shouldn't be.*
> Tom Bromly, Artist

Beech Trees, Scotland. Oil on canvas. Tom Bromly.

Battlefield and Trees. Oil on canvas. Tom Bromly.

Britain's first cross-border Ecomuseum links together twelve sites across North Northumberland, the Scottish Borders and Edinburgh.

These sites are all connected to the story of Flodden.

They are captured here at 9am on the day of the 500th anniversary: 9 September 2013. (9am on the 9th of the 9th)

Flodden Field

Norham Castle

Etal Castle

Weetwood Bridge

Ladykirk Church

Heatherslaw Mill

Twizel Bridge

Coldstream Museum

The Flodden Wall

Fletcher Monument

Barmoor Castle

Branxton Church

Solvitur Ambulando

Peace Pilgrims from both sides of the border walk in the footsteps of soldiers, wearing white T-shirts instead of chest plates and carrying peace banners in place of swords.

We are reversing the darkness, bringing light to the darkness.

Roy Searle, Pilgrim

How do I live as a person of peace in a violent world?

Paul Revill, Pilgrim

We've been trying to reflect on what the soldiers would have felt – I think a bit of excitement but a lot of fear.

David Pott, Pilgrim

The Solemn Commemoration welcomed towns from both sides of the border to gather and reflect on the battle as friends instead of enemies.

Hundreds of people – including soldiers' descendants from all over the world – came to commemorate their ancestors at this ceremony.

Music and traditions from both cultures mixed harmoniously.

I've heard the lilting, at the yowe-milking,
Lassies a-lilting before dawn o' day;
But now they are moaning on ilka green loaning;
"The Floo'ers o' the Forest are a' wede away".

Jean Elliot, *The Floo'ers o' the Forest*

Credits

Students

David Ayre
Photography, photo editing, filming, film editing

Anna Dakin
Photography, photo editing, sketches and paintings, layout design

Alistair Herd
Photography, photo editing and other image manipulation

Emily Lerpiniere
Photography, writing, text editing

Jack Robertson
Photography, filming, film editing

Joe Sanders
Photography, writing, text editing

Nathaniel Williams
Photography, filming, film editing and other moving-image manipulation

Special thanks to

Heritage Lottery Fund
Berwick Academy
Coldstream Pipe Band
Martins The Printers
Flodden 1513 Ecomuseum
Ford & Etal Estates

Alistair Bowden
Jozsef Brandon
Chris Burgess
Becki Cooper
Clare Dakin
George Farr
Oliver & Jamie Farr
The Earl of Home
Barbara & John Huddart
Lord Joicey
Rob Kelsey
Colin MacConnachie
Frank Mansfield
Lynda McCraw
Alan Mills
The Duke of Norfolk
Haroon Rashid
Ian Shields
Derek James Stewart
Tom Thomson
Peter & Amanda Warlock
John White

Published by Blackhall Publishing, Sea View Works, Spittal, Berwick-upon-Tweed, TD15 1RS, on behalf of the Flodden 1513 Ecomuseum, c/o The Estate Office, Ford, Berwick-upon-Tweed TD15 2QA (www.flodden1513.com)

ISBN: 978-0-9576187-2-5